THE SEA OF CHANGE

Solutions for Navigating the
Disconnects in the Workplace

by Judy I. Suiter

PO Box 2418
Peachtree City, GA 30269
www.competitiveedgeinc.com

The Sea of Change: Solutions for Navigating the
Disconnects in the Workplace

Copyright 2008, Judy I. Suiter
Published by Competitive Edge, Inc

Design, illustrations and typography by Anoleworks

Photographs: istockphoto.com

Printed in the United States of America

First Edition, 2008

ISBN: 978-0-981-5252-0-4

DEDICATION

~To my newest grandchild, Sydney Ann Suiter and for
my International Clients who continue to inspire me~

Acknowledgments

When one sits down to write a book or any other type of publication, the work is not done in solitude. Over time, many, many people have contributed their ideas, thoughts, stories and experiences to what the writer is trying to convey. This book is no different; I have many people to acknowledge for what they have done for me and my organization, for the lessons they have taught me, and what they tell me they need in the way of information and instruction.

First and foremost, I thank my clients and associates who continue to support me in numerous ways. To Bill Brockwell, Bruce Clements, Joe Miller, Diane Evans, Allison Khroustalev, Nancy Thornton, Tricia Wade, Jerry Nagel, Rick West, Dr. David Davis, Kim Walton, Hope Cheeks and Jesyka Simpson, I extend my heartfelt thanks. I would be remiss if I did not acknowledge Ken Bratz, Ann Minton, Krista Sheets, Aben and Tammy Gentry, Hank and Patrice Humphrey, Dean and Pam Gentry, Alberta Lloyd, Sharlene Alexander, Darbie Bufford, Lynne Snead, Chuck Kruger, Frank Molinario, Laura Daigle, Marie Kane, Joan Smith, Bill Allen, George Myers, Marie Dodd, Peggy Baker, Cindy Neskie, Mark Welker and Bridgette Drelling. Your support, advice and assistance are immeasurable. Thank you to the former managers and employees of the Ford Motor Company plant in Hapeville, Georgia for giving me my very first big team building contract.

To the group I refer to as my Preferred Suppliers, Bill Bonnstetter and TTI, Jeff Sugarman, Barry Davis, Julie Straw and the rest of the Inscape staff, Ira Wolfe of

Success Performance Solutions, Bill Schult of Maximum Potential, Jim Cecil of the James P. Cecil Company, Dudley and Sherry Lynch of Brain Technologies and Bobby Foster of Organizer Plus, I sincerely thank you for what you do that complements my work.

Of course, my office staff and friends who continue to nurture me and who always challenge me to reach beyond my limits and move to the next plateau deserve my heartfelt appreciation. Janet Boyce, who assists me in my research and writing, Mary Lacombe, my steadfast and loyal Customer Service Manager and Sonya Boggs, my efficient and creative Office Manager and Executive Assistant, all continue to provide invaluable contributions to the successes of Competitive Edge, Inc. Then there is Eileen Tooley, my longtime associate, who keeps my financial side running smoothly, and Mark Goodall, my IT support person, who keeps my computers up and running. Thanks to my longtime friends, Patricia Colston and Bertha Morel. I can always count on both of you.

Finally, to my family, you are the light of my life. Without you, I would not have the passion to do what I do. To Brett and Keely, Drew and Karen, and my grandchildren, Blake and Sydney, I love you all. To my sister Linda and her husband Glenn, thanks for sharing my life's journey.

So, in essence, this book came to fruition from many sources. If I neglected to mention anyone, I'll catch you in my next book!

TABLE OF CONTENTS

Dedication

Acknowledgements

Introduction

Absenteeism   **1**

    -Absenteeism Caused by Substance Abuse   **7**

Communication   **13**

Connectivity   **17**

Employee Engagement   **21**

Employee Retention/Turnover   **25**

Entitlement   **31**

Ethical Issues   **35**

Generational Differences   **39**

Skills Gap   **45**

Trust   **51**

Work/Life Balance   **55**

Workplace Readiness   **59**

Workplace Stress   **63**

Change Agents   **69**

Something Extra   **79**

Recommended Resources   **81**

About the Author   **83**

Introduction

How many of you feel we are inundated with text messaging, ubiquitous e-mails, journals/books and overall information and data that just seem to overwhelm us? We ask ourselves, "How do we make sense of it all, what is important and what is just plain irrelevant?" When I sat down to think about how to deal with this information overload I, of course, analyzed it from my viewpoint as a training consultant to major organizations, and immediately decided that in this book I would focus on what I deal with the most – people and their roles in an organization.

One of the things I look at as I prepare any type of training is how well the company handles their employees. Not all companies look at human capital as an asset; most organizations tend to treat it as one large item in the expense column. Mark Welker, one of my associates, always says, "The problems are always in the numbers, the solutions are always in the people." I, too, believe that the problems or successes associated with any organization can be traced to the employees or what we call human capital. They are the organizers, the producers, the problem solvers, our interface with customers, and ultimately the final effect on the bottom line. They hold the key to any successes or failures of all organizations. Geoffrey Colvin, the senior editor at large for Fortune magazine puts it this way, "Financial capital is no longer the scarce resource in business. Human capital is the key to winning."

We have already entered into one of the biggest challenges facing organizations in this period of history with regard to having a workforce who is skilled, knowledgeable and resourceful. Employers are looking for people who possess a strong work ethic, who are self-motivated and goal-oriented. Warren Buffet sees it this way: "When hiring someone, I look for integrity, knowledge and energy and if they don't have the first one, the other two will kill you!" The implications of finding employees with these qualifications will reverberate throughout all industries in the United States as well as globally as we all seek workers to fill positions within our organizations. This became very apparent to me in the fall of 2006, when I personally witnessed a large Chinese contingency recruiting for seasoned managers in Luxembourg. (The reality is the Chinese have millions of workers but are sorely lacking in managers who are effective and have leadership ability.) To compete for qualified workers, we must be fully cognizant of what it takes to win and retain the best.

In order to do that, we need to create a benchmark identifying the skills required to do the job for the position we are attempting to fill. Once on board, the next step is to integrate them into the company culture, train them adequately and reward them appropriately. We must make certain that they operate in an ethical manner, show up for work, and leave any entitlement attitude they may possess behind. Employers now and in the future must identify key performance indicators for each job and communicate those expectations to their employees in a timely and efficient manner in order to ensure the quality of the products or services. However, what I am finding from all the research data is that there is a huge disconnect within what is needed and what is actually happening.

Most of the information in this book has been known for years and has been fully supported by empirical research data, articles and books. We are constantly being told that people are our most important asset. So why, presently, do the majority of employees feel they are not valued by their employer? The reason is that top executives in most organizations got there the hard way, and they want everyone else to do the same. That thinking will not work today as younger workers with different work expectations and goals are entering the workforce and changing how work gets done. Like it or not, this is happening! Our job, then, becomes even more challenging. Jack Welch's take on hiring is this, "If we don't get the people thing right, we lose; it is the most important thing in our business."

So, how does our search for the best available talent fit with the above information overload? It is my intent that this book will cut through the massive amounts of statistics and information surrounding workplace issues as we identify the key challenges facing organizations along with supporting statistics. You will also note a section within each challenge which I call "the disconnect," that I noted above. Finally, I will attempt to offer my solutions.

This book has been intentionally kept small and concise. With this model in mind, I believe you will be able to find not only the statistics, but the solution to your workplace challenges quickly and easily. Because change is a constant in our lives, I have titled this book, "The Sea of Change." The title aligns itself with earlier books I have published as they all have nautical or water themes. We can drown in a sea of change or we can seek solutions. I choose the latter.

~ ABSENTEEISM ~

OH, WHAT EXCUSES WE USE...

~ "I accidentally flushed my keys down the toilet."

~ "I couldn't find anything to wear."

~ "My electricity went out and my alarm didn't go off."

~ "My house lock jammed, and I'm locked in."

~ "I was out too late last night."

~ "I thought it was Saturday."

~ "My car battery died."

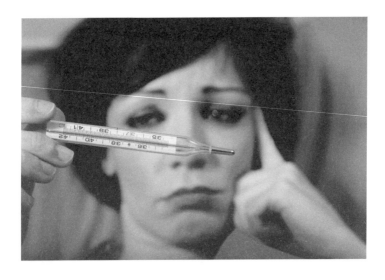

"In these matters the only certainty is that nothing is certain."

~Pliny the Elder (23 AD-79AD)

~ ABSENTEEISM ~

Definition: The failure to show up; an employee who is not on the job during scheduled working hours, except for a granted leave of absence, holiday or vacation time.

Absenteeism is a chronic problem that continues to eat away at organizational excellence. In a recent *Business Week* article, it was reported that hourly workers in auto plants often don't show up for work. In the auto industry, absenteeism runs 10% a year, three times higher than in other industries. In fact, General Motors is considering adding this to their new union contract: Workers could win a new car if they have perfect attendance. This is very telling evidence on how large a problem absenteeism has become within organizations.

The Situation according to the 2005 CCH Unscheduled Absence Survey:

- 31% of employers report absenteeism to be a serious problem
- 67% of employees who fail to show up aren't physically ill
- 92% of employers think the problem may stay the same or worsen in the next two years, up from 7% in 2005

- Companies lose approximately 2.8 million work-days each year - 3 to 6% of any given workforce is absent every day due to unscheduled issues or disability claims
- While the rate of unscheduled absenteeism has barely budged since 2005, the average per employee costs has risen to $660 per employee, costing some $60,000 per year for small employers while costing over $850,000 for larger organizations
- The absenteeism rate was 2.5% in 2006, up from 2.3% in 2005, and the highest since 1999, when the rate was 2.7%
- Companies with low morale say absenteeism is twice as high as those at organizations with Good/ Very Good morale
- Employers set aside an average of 5.8% of their budgets for absenteeism. When morale is factored in, organizations with Poor/Fair projected 6.2% of their budgets to cover absenteeism costs
- Personal illness accounts for only 33% of unscheduled absences down from 43% in 2005; family issues accounts for 24%; personal needs, 18%; stress, 12% and entitlement mentality was 11%
- Additional costs are lost productivity, morale, missed deadlines, lost sales and temporary labor costs
- Tardiness is another form of absenteeism that is rapidly growing

The Disconnect:

- 23% of the workers said they just wanted to relax and catch up on sleep
- 17% said they just didn't feel like going in

- 16% said they had a doctor's excuse
- 9% said they had to catch up on housework and run personal errands
- 38% said they viewed sick days as equivalent to vacation days
- The most popular day for calling in sick was Wednesday with 27% of workers getting over the mid-week hump by fabricating an excuse
- 26% of workers called in sick on Monday and 14% on Friday
- 63% of hiring managers said they are more suspicious of employees calling in sick on a Monday or a Friday

The Solution:

- Better hiring techniques that match employees' behaviors, values and skills for the right job fit
- Pre-employment assessments such as the *Counterproductive Behavior Index or Candid Clues* to determine workplace attitudes that the potential candidate may have toward drug or alcohol use, absenteeism, theft and lying, aggression, sexual harassment and computer abuse
- Increased communications between management/ employees to help employees feel they are valued and that their job is important
- Be sure that all personnel policies are in written form and are communicated to all employees as part of new employee orientation.

- Initiating a Work-Life Balance Program that may include Employee Assistance Plans, Leave for School Functions, Wellness Programs, Flu Shot Programs, a Fitness Facility, Telecommuting, a Compressed Work Week and Child Care on Site. Many companies are also adopting a Concierge Program that provides services such as errand "running" to pickup dry-cleaning or having employees' cars serviced. (U.S. companies now offer an average of 11 work-life programs, up from nine in 2005 and eight in 2004)
- Eliminate the situation of stress-related absenteeism being caused by authoritarian management styles or by poor employee relationships through training in interpersonal skills
- Make more efficient use of absence-control programs already in place that include such procedures as verification of illness, yearly review, and disciplinary action. Learn to say "no." Make certain employees are following leave policies
- Initiate Buy-Back programs that enable the employee to receive cash or vacation time for unused sick time and Paid Leave Banks that allow employees to use time off for reasons other than illness Introduce a reward system for any improvement to sick leave rates
- Recognize a developing problem and intervene early before it escalates through the use of a neutral third party in-house mediator

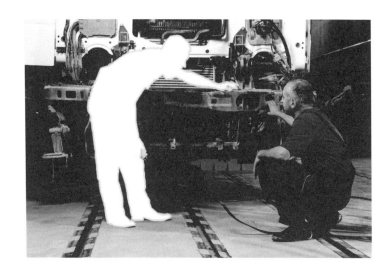

"A man too busy to take care of his health is like a
mechanic too busy to take care of his tools."

~Spanish proverb

~ ABSENTEEISM CAUSED BY
SUBSTANCE ABUSE ~

❖ "Boss talking productivity
It's a sin to fall behind
I'm wondering should I walk away
Lose my job or lose my mind."

Song, *"Nothing but the Same Old Story"*
by Paul Brady and Christy Moore

❖ "I'm gettin' paid by the hour, and older by the
minute. My boss just pushed me over the limit."

Song, *"It's Five O' Clock Somewhere"*
by Jimmy Buffett

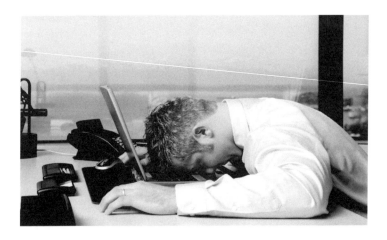

"A bend in the road is not the end of the road...unless you fail to make the turn."

~R. E. Rufing

~ ABSENTEEISM CAUSED BY SUBSTANCE ABUSE ~

Definition of Substance Abuse: The overindulgence in and dependence upon an addictive substance such as alcohol or narcotic drugs. Illicit drug use is defined as the use of marijuana/hashish, cocaine, heroin, hallucinogens, or inhalants, or prescription drugs used non-medically. Heavy alcohol use is defined as drinking five or more drinks on the same occasion on five or more days in the past 30 days.

Many organizations say, "Substance abuse isn't a problem here. We would notice it if it were." But, actually what is occurring in workplaces everywhere is that many of their employees ARE using drugs and alcohol which results in huge costs to both the individual and the organization. Substance abuse IS occurring within the workplace at alarming rates.

The Situation:

- 68% of all illegal drug users are employed full or part-time
- An estimated 9 million workers are substance abusers
- 20% of all employees, ages 18-25 years and 13% of all employees ages 26-34 years uses drugs on the job

- More than 15% of Americans employed full and part-time, or 19.2 million workers, report heavy drinking. The heaviest drinking occurred among persons between the ages of 18-25 years. Of the 11.2 million heavy drinkers in 1997, 30% or 3.3 million also were current illicit drug users
- 60% of alcohol-related work performance problems can be attributed to employees who are not alcohol dependent, but who occasionally drink too much on a work night or drink during a weekday lunch
- 23% of upper management and 11% of first-line supervisors report having drinks during the workday compared to 8% of hourly workers
- 5 million of the country's estimated employed substance abusers work for small companies as they tend to hire younger workers who make up the age group with the largest percentage of substance abuse
- A survey of callers to the National Cocaine Helpline revealed that 75% reported using drugs on the job, while 64% said that drugs adversely affected their job performance
- An estimated 500 million workdays are lost annually to alcoholism while problems related to substance abuse cost American businesses $100 billion in lost productivity every year
- Employers experience a 300% increase in their medical costs and benefits because of substance abusers
- Up to 40% of industrial fatalities and 47% of industrial injuries can be linked to alcohol consumption and alcoholism

- 21% of workers reported being injured or put in danger, having to re-do work or to cover for a co-workers, or needing to work harder because of others' drinking
- 75% of hourly workers at one manufacturing plant reported that it was easy for them to drink at their work stations. These employees were assembly line workers, electricians and machinists according to the National Council on Alcoholism and Drug Dependence

The Disconnect:

- Substance abusers are:
    - 5 times more likely to file a worker's compensation claim
    - 3.6 times more likely to be involved in a workplace accident
    - 2.5 times more likely to have lengthy absences from work
    - 3 times more likely to be late for work
    - Likely to use 2.5 times more medical benefits
    - 1/3 less productive
    - More likely to sell drugs to other employees
    - More likely to steal from co-workers to support their habits
    - More than twice as likely to have changed employers three or more times in the past year
- Less than one-third of 1% of employed persons are receiving treatment for alcoholism and other drug dependence

The Solution:

- Conduct a pre-employment assessment such as *Candid Clues* to determine workplace attitudes that potential candidates may have toward drugs or alcohol use
- Establish a mandatory drug testing policy
- Provide Employee Assistance Programs (EAPs) that offer education, information on treatment centers, and short-term confidential counseling. It is estimated for every dollar an employer invests in an EAP, the savings range from $5 to $16 in reduced absenteeism, improved productivity and a safer work environment
- Communicate with new hires immediately and with all employees often and continually
- Be aware of stress symptoms that employees may exhibit that may lead to drug use. Symptoms may include frequent irritation, procrastination, anger, and/or listlessness.
- Conduct workshops using the *Coping and Stress Profile®* to help reduce employee problematic symptoms.

"We can't wait for the storm to blow over, we've got to learn to work in the rain."

~Pete Silas
Chairman, Phillips Petroleum

~ COMMUNICATION ~

"I HEARD IT THROUGH THE GRAPEVINE..."

"If you don't give people information, they'll make up something to fill the void."

~Carla O'Dell

"The most important thing in communication is to hear what isn't being said."

~Peter Drucker

"When facts are few, opinions loom large."

~Karl Jung

"If you want others to care about what you say---care about what they have to say!"

~Marshall Goldsmith

~ COMMUNICATION ~

Definition: The exchange of thoughts, messages or information by the use of speech, signals, writing or behavior.

Communication is often spoken of as the "skill that separates." When we communicate improperly, the separation becomes a chasm that, once created, is often hard, even impossible to cross. How we say it and what we actually mean are too often in conflict with each other, but we all realize that communication skills are the key to any successful relationship. George Bernard Shaw writes, "The biggest problem in communication is the illusion that it has been accomplished."

The Situation:

- The financial performance of organizations that are perceived as good communicators by employees is more than twice the financial performance of organizations perceived with poor communications (Work USA Study)
- A mere 37% of management explain decisions well (Work USA Study)
- Companies with high integrity also have a 74% rate for seeking employee suggestions

- 62% of companies cite strong verbal and written communications as one of the most important skills employees must have (Randstad's 2005 Employee Review)
- When asked what they would do if they became president of their companies, 17% said they would work to improve employee communication (Robert Half Management Resources)
- Clear communication is the most effective tool for eliminating fear, which staffing professional Eva Jenkins says is the dominant characteristic of the 21st century
- 15% of an employee's work time is wasted every year because of miscommunication
- 55% of communication is non-verbal, 38% comes from the voice tone and 7% is from the actual words used or spoken

The Disconnect:

- Just 30% of companies involve employees in decisions that affect them while 81% of respondents to a Ken Blanchard survey report that leaders fail to listen to or involve others in the process
- Companies with low integrity have only a 5% rate for seeking employee suggestions (Watson Wyatt Study)
- A whopping 68% of companies provide training to entry level workers to raise basic skills that includes communication
- Poor communication regarding organizational goals is an important obstacle preventing delivery of operational excellence (Randstad)

The Solution:

- On-going training in communication skills for management and employees that teaches how to communicate with different behavioral styles and values perspectives. Recommendation is to use TTI *Success Insights* assessments as part of the training programs
- Learn to listen to your employees' concerns and provide ample opportunities for employees to discuss workplace issues with management
- Greater proficiency in the use of e-mails, bulletin boards, and newsletters to promote effective communications and a sense of belonging
- Management should be more visible, do more "walk-a-rounds," engage employees in conversation and ask more questions to get their input and make them feel valued
- Employee surveys to evaluate employee/employer and employee/employee communication effectiveness within the organization
- Schedule lunches with corporate executives and small groups of employees to have informal discussions of their concerns

~ CONNECTIVITY ~

"Consider the following. We humans are social beings. We come into the world as the result of others' actions. We survive here in dependence on others. Whether we like it or not, there is hardly a moment of our lives when we do not benefit from others' activities. For this reason it is hardly surprising that most of our happiness arises in the context of our relationships with others."

~The Dalai Lama

"I sense an insatiable demand for connectivity. ...
Perhaps some of them feel hungry for a community
that our real neighborhoods don't deliver..."

~Clifford Stoll

~ CONNECTIVITY ~

Definition: The pragmatic definition refers to the unbiased transport of packets between two end points which is closely related to the theory of network flow problems. However, when dealing with human capital issues we are referring to face-to-face interactions. Think of connectivity as the human touch within a technological world.

The Situation:

When employees have a best friend at work, the following occurs:

- Their work engagement increases more than seven times what it would be without the friend relationship
- They have fewer accidents
- There is a lower turnover rate and a safer environment
- They also have more engaged customers
- Employees are more likely to be innovative and share ideas
- With three close friends at work, employees are 96% more likely to be very satisfied with their lives and are 46% more likely to experience job satisfaction

- Women have more friends at work than do men – 33% versus 25%
- According to author, Malcolm Gladwell, a friend at work acts as a connector to a network
- Workers would choose to have a best friend at work over a 10% pay raise
- While stress is still experienced, talking it out reduces the intensity

The Disconnect:

- Just 30% of employees interviewed say they have a best friend at work
- Only 18% of people work for organizations that encourage friendships on job
- The number of people with no confidante in any area of their lives rose from 10% in 1985 to almost 25% in 2004
- The Gallup Organization Survey found that just 8% of those without a good work pal are engaged in their jobs; 63% are not engaged, and 29% are actively disengaged

The Solution:

- Use a customized survey or an assessment such as the *Work Expectations Profile*® to measure employee engagement and morale
- Provide regular and meaningful activities/ assignments that foster a spirit of teamwork
- Provide mentoring to new employees
- When hiring, a "connector" or one who has

many friends and makes friends easily, helps to foster employee relationships

- Quarterly "employee get-togethers" after work hours
- Sponsor sports programs such as bowling teams, softball, golf, tennis, etc.
- Hold breakfast or lunch meetings with company leaders to answer questions and to keep employees informed about the financial wellness of the company

~ EMPLOYEE ENGAGEMENT ~

WE'VE LOST THAT LOVING FEELING...

~ Unhappy, disengaged workers are expensive.

~ It should be showtime, but it's not.

~ Purpose matters.

~ Lost opportunity, lost productivity, lost customers.

"I give 100% to my job every week: 15% on Monday, 25% on Tuesday, 35% on Wednesday, 20% on Thursday, and 5% on Friday!"
~From the Vent column, Atlanta Journal-Constitution, 10/04/07

"When you have disciplined people, you don't need hierarchy. When you have disciplined thought, you don't need bureaucracy. When you have disciplined action, you don't need excessive controls."

~Jim Collins, *Good to Great*

~ EMPLOYEE ENGAGEMENT ~

Definition: A heightened emotional connection that an employee feels for his or her organization, that influences him or her to exert greater discretionary effort to his or her work. (Conference Board)

The Situation:

- Engaged workers makeup a mere 26% of the American workplace, are more committed to the organization and accept accountability and responsibility for their actions
- Engaged workers are far more likely to suggest or develop creative ways to improve management or business processes
- Companies with higher levels of employee engagement outperformed the S&P by 24% over a three-year span
- Engaged workers are more likely to find creative ways to solve customer problems or involve their customers in creating service innovation (Gallup Study 2006)

The Disconnect:

- What takes an employee all week to do could be done in 60% of the time according to a University of Michigan study
- In the average organization, according to the Gallup Organization, 74% of all employees are either unengaged or actively disengaged workers, operating at only two-thirds capacity, resulting in about one-third of the company's payroll wasted
- 22 million U.S. workers are actively disengaged, are not risk takers, and have a low commitment to the organization
- Only about one-third of an average organization's workers are loyal while the other two-thirds feel trapped in their jobs and are planning on leaving
- The cost of lost productivity from disengaged workers is $287 to $370 billion per year to the U.S. economy
- Disengaged workers are more likely to be dissatisfied with both work and their personal lives
- Disengaged workers are not results-oriented and usually perform at a minimum level just high enough to keep their jobs and tend to miss an average of 3.5 more days per year than engaged workers
- Unengaged, but talented employees are in the wrong job

The Solution:

- Use a customized survey such as the *Work Expectations Profile* to determine the degree of employee engagement

- Provide management and/or leadership skills training because you can hire the right person with the right skills for the job, but if they are not managed effectively, they will experience increase health problems or they will leave
- Some of the skills required for effective leadership and/or management are understanding yourself, recognizing others' behavioral styles and values, and being to able to adapt your style and values to be more effective. Recommend *Success Insights Reports* to determine employees and managers styles and values
- Lead by example
- Hire for the appropriate job and provide ongoing training and potential career growth steps
- Show appreciation for employees' progress and improvement by providing incentives/rewards
- Provide challenges along with appropriate work expectation

~ EMPLOYEE RETENTION/TURNOVER ~

COMMENTS OVERHEARD FROM EMPLOYEES/EMPLOYERS:

~ "It was all about the bottom line. Get as much blood out of the stone that you can." [An employee quoting an employer's philosophy on workers]

~ "Appreciation day is just a free lunch, nothing more. No 'attaboys,' no mention of 'I appreciate how you got the last shipment out.' That free lunch really puts me over the top!"

~ "I really don't feel valued by my employer."

"The grass is not, in fact, always greener on the other side of the fence. Fences have nothing to do with it. The grass is greenest where it is watered. When crossing over fences, carry water with you and tend the grass wherever you may be."

~Robert Fulghum,
It Was on Fire When I Lay Down on It

~ EMPLOYEE RETENTION/TURNOVER ~

Definition of employee retention: The effort by an employer to keep desirable workers in order to meet business objectives.

Definition of employee turnover: The unplanned loss of workers who <u>voluntarily</u> <u>leave</u> and whom employers would like to retain, while <u>involuntary</u> <u>turnover</u> consists of those who are poor performers, violators of company policies, participants in illegal activities and the like who are asked to leave.

The Situation:

- According to the most recent surveys, CEOs of the fastest growing companies identified employee retention as the most critical factor in planning for the year ahead
- A recent survey of more than 14,000 employees and human resources managers found that 65% of workers planned to be job hunting in the coming year. (Compensation Consultancy Salary)

- The U.S. Bureau of Labor Statistics reports that 26 million Americans will retire from the 147 million-person labor force by 2008
- *Business 2.0*, May 2006, reports that job openings have increased by almost 500,000 since the summer of 2005
- In their January 2005 study, Input of Reston Virginia projected that by 2008, 45% of the federal government's information technology workers would be 50 years of age or older
- Peter Fasolo's study for Bristol-Myers shows that nine out of the top ten factors which influence employees of Bristol-Meyers to stay are influenced by their managers, and no other reasons
- In Randstad's 2005 Employee Review Study, 72% of respondents rate job security as one of the top aspects that would persuade them to stay on the job, while 80% says that job satisfaction is most important for staying on the job
- 91% of 391 U.S. based firms report that turnover remained stubbornly high or worsened during 2005

The Disconnect:

High employee turnover results in:
- An estimated $5 trillion expense annually to the U.S. economy
- Reduced organizational earnings as high as 38%
- Decreased customer loyalty and profitability
- Less loyalty to employer and vice versa
- Lower employee morale
- A loss of trust in leadership because of ethical lapses, layoffs, off-shoring

- Organizational knowledge walks out the door when talented and qualified workers leave
- Fewer qualified employees available for promotion

The Solution:

- Do the right thing; be ethical
- Put the right person in the right position with better hiring techniques using assessments along with proper new-hire orientation. A 2005 survey by Leadership IQ shows the five major reasons new hires fail:
  - 26% can't accept feedback
  - 23% can't understand and manage emotions
  - 17% lack necessary motivation
  - 15% possess wrong temperament
  - 11% lack technical competence
- Provide employees with challenging and meaningful work
- Mentoring/coaching programs that focus on engagement and retention for new employees or those who need additional training
- Ongoing essential training with appropriate feedback
- Flexible work arrangements or telecommuting when possible
- Pay adjustments that align with the market's current pay scale
- Replace annual reviews with semiannual or ongoing reviews to provide greater efficacy with employee concerns/ performance

- Stock awards, 401k programs and/or profit-sharing plans
- Retention bonuses
- Work to retain top performers within your organization by asking what would make them stay, providing opportunities for growth within the organization
- Provide a work environment that is stable and congenial, where employees work together, are respected and feel valued
- Convey a sense of trust by ongoing communication
- Listen to what your employees are saying
- Conduct Effective Listening Workshop using the *Personal Listening Profile®* by Inscape Publishing
- Be visible and accessible to your employees
- Have exit interviews conducted by outside source
- Use behavioral and values assessments to help both employers understand their employees and vice versa. Recommended assessment is *Success Insights*
- To identify what behavioral style is required for a specific job, use *Success Insights Work Environment Profile* to benchmark the job

"If we don't get the people thing right, we lose; it is the most important thing in our business."

~Jack Welch

~ ENTITLEMENT ~

WHISPERS FROM THE BREAKROOM:

"Many workers believe that they are deserving of better positions, more perks, and higher pay without paying their dues."

A new hire asks his manager, "How long will I be in this position before being promoted?"

"It took me twenty years to get where I am, and they want what??"

"I want it NOW!"

They do not mean to do harm ... they are absorbed in the endless struggle to think well of themselves."

~ T. S. Eliot

~ ENTITLEMENT ~

Definition: It is an attitude, a way of looking at life that is displayed by people who believe that they do not have to earn what they get. They believe that they get something because they are owed it, they are entitled to it, and because of whom they are not because of what they do. (Note: this section is not to be confused with those policies that protect workers' rights and jobs.)

The Situation:

- Where entitlement attitudes are allowed to exist, the only solutions are more entitlements
- In organizations where entitlement prevails, after a crisis passes the entitlement mode returns
- No organization can afford to carry unproductive people in such a highly competitive market
- Entitlement mentality is expected to rise as lean staffing continues
- 55% of workers surveyed believe that many employees act as if they are more deserving than others at work without "paying their dues"
- Employees ages 30 and younger report more perceived entitlement than employees ages 50 and older
- Younger employees report 50% more job tension when co-workers act entitled

The Disconnect:

When present, **entitlement**:
- Destroys motivation
- Creates an environment of distrust
- Prevents efficient and harmonious teamwork
- Lowers productivity, encourages non-performance
- Crushes self-esteem
- Creates complacency
- Gives no incentive to work hard
- Institutionalizes security
- Requires many rules and bureaucracy to sustain it
- Creates apathy as empathy is diminished
- Encourages "looking busy" rather than "being busy"
- Overall, leads to workplace tensions

The Solution:

- Provide assessments such as *Work Expectations Profile* to determine the level of employee engagement
- Training in Team Building skills
- Establish focus groups to open discussion among employees and with managers/supervisors
- Foster an environment in which all employees are empowered, engaged and feel that their contributions are needed and worthwhile
- Create benchmarks and performance targets that can be measured and evaluated on a regular basis

"The great majority of people tend to focus downward. They are occupied with efforts rather than results. They worry over what the organization and their superiors 'owe' them and should do for them. And they are conscious, above all, of the authority they 'should have.' As a result they render themselves ineffectual."

~Peter Drucker

~ ETHICAL ISSUES ~

Recent headlines...

~CEO of telecom firm is found guilty on 19 of 42 counts of insider trading

~More firms rocked by allegations of backdating of stock-options

~Corruption rife in international business

~Seven former executives charged in a $3 billion accounting scheme

~Hard-hitting ethics attorney general elected governor forced to resign because of indiscriminate activities

~Mayor of major U.S. city charged with eight-count criminal indictment that includes 6 felony charges

"There is no such thing as business ethics – there is only ethics."

~Peter Drucker

~ ETHICAL ISSUES ~

Definition of ethics: The principles of conduct governing an individual or a group that involve moral issues such as good/bad, right/wrong, and beneficial/harmful.

FACTORS MOST LIKELY TO CAUSE EMPLOYEES TO CROSS ETHICAL LINES (in order of rank)

- Pressure to meet unrealistic objectives/deadlines
- Desire to further career
- Desire to protect one's livelihood
- Working in an environment with low morale
- Improper training/ignorance of ethical issues
- No consequence if caught
- Need to follow boss's orders
- Peer pressure/desire to be team player
- To harm or steal from organization
- To help organization survive
- To save their job
- Because of a sense of loyalty

(KPMG Study)

The Situation:

A 2000 survey of corporate workers found:
- 56% said companies used deceptive practices with customers

- Nearly 33% said quality and safety tests were altered or falsified
- Almost 33% said antitrust violations or unfair competitive practices were used
- However, 77% of new MBA recipients want potential employers to be ethically bound, while 97% want employers to be above reproach

(The Sarbannes-Oxley Act of 2002, passed to restore ethical practices and tighter internal controls, costs U.S. businesses over $6.1 billion to comply.)

The Disconnect:

- The average U.S. company loses 6% of its annual revenue to internal malfeasance, ranging from fraudulent financial statements to kickbacks extorted from suppliers
- Top executives skimmed off the most: $900,000 per person and committed 12% of all wrongdoing
- Managers pocketed $140,000 per person in 12% of all wrongdoing
- Ordinary employees took $62,000 per person in 68% of all cases
- Just 68% of organizations train employees in compliance, while only 55% had oversight (2004 Study by Association of Certified Fraud Examiners)
- A mere 46% of 1,800 communications professionals said that their organizations encouraged discussions of ethical/unethical behavior, while just 51% said that unethical behavior that results in corporate gain is reprimanded
- A study of 5,300 MBA students revealed that 56% have academically cheated

- 57% of hiring managers say they have found discrepancies on a candidate's application
- Just 5% admit to lying about their academic background

The Solution:

- Despite the current trend towards ethics training, human nature, being what it is, demands that modeling is the prime motivator of proper ethical behavior
- Set the ethics bar high
- Make ethics part of the training and development process through the use of DVDs such as *Act with Integrity*
- Use real life case studies in training programs to teach acceptable ethical behavior
- Communicate what is acceptable/unacceptable within your organization
- Give more than lip service to your organization's code of ethics. Model it daily through consistent and principled actions
- Eliminate all actions that could be seen as a double standard
- Get rid of tainted employees from top to bottom

~ GENERATIONAL DIFFERENCES ~

THE TIMES THEY ARE A CHANGING...

Come gather round people wherever you roam
And admit that the waters around you have grown
And accept it that soon you'll be drenched to the bone
If your time to you is worth saving
Then you'd better start swimming or you'll sink like a stone
For the times, they are a changing

~Bob Dylan

"Strange how the older generations can't program a VCR/ DVD if their life depended on it, but they managed to operate the climate control system of their 1958 Ramblers which consisted of six unmarked knobs, one labeled "AirFloMatic" in unreadable cursive script, and four levers underneath the dash, which you had to turn, then pull."

~Dan Tasman

"Long ago, the Native Americans of the Great Plains survived the harsh winters by having grandparents and grandchildren sleep beside each other to keep from freezing to death. That is a good metaphor for what the generations do for each other. The old need our heat, and we need their light."
~Mary Pipher, quoted in Reader's Digest, October 2000

~ GENERATIONAL DIFFERENCES ~

Definition: The generational diversity that exists in society, in the workplace or among its client, customer or supplier base. These differences influence working and societal relationships, standards of behavior, how work is viewed, values and beliefs, world views, expectations and how success is measured.

- Traditionalists – born between 1900 and 1945 and number about 75 million people
- The Baby Boomers – born between 1946 and 1964 and number about 80 million people
- Generation Xers – born between 1965 and 1980 and number about 46 million
- Millennials (Gen Y) – born between 1981 and 1999 and number 76 million

The Situation:

- Traditionalists comprise over 40% of the U. S. labor force and tend to stay with one organization for longer periods of time than do the other generational groups

- By 2010, two employees will be leaving for every new hire entering as the Boomers retire
- Boomers currently dominate the ranks of upper management
- Generation Xers value individualism and self-reliance
- Millennials are multi-taskers who are technically savvy, globally-oriented and prefer a fun-type/fast paced working environment
- Generation Xers and Millennials bring a different viewpoint to the workplace as they usually had both parents in the workplace whom they view as being overworked and sometimes unemployed because of corporate downsizing
- Boomers are more likely to be work-centered than other generations as over 22% are work-centric compared to 12 to 13% of other generations
- College-educated Generation Xers and Millennials would prefer to work fewer hours and are 40% less likely to want to take on more job responsibilities
- 75% of workers 55 and over say they relate well to younger co-workers
- About 10% of workers 40 and older are retirees who have returned to the workforce (Putnam Investment Study)

The Disconnect:

- 77% of experienced workers say younger employees do not seek advice from them (Randstad)
- Just 23% of younger workers believe older workers bring fresh ideas to the workplace
- Approximately 44% of all workers say they do not

relate well to older co-workers (Randstad)
- Younger workers resent the inability to move ahead because of what they call the "Gray Ceiling"
- Replacing experienced workers can cost at least 50% of an individual's annual salary, even more with specialized jobs
- 79% of Baby Boomers plan to work in some capacity after formal retirement
- Work styles are different for each generation as Traditionalists believe in following "the book," Baby Boomers "do whatever it takes," Generation Xers want results and quickly, while Millennials will work to deadlines, not necessarily to schedules
- The communication style for Traditionalists is formal through proper channels, for Baby Boomers, less formal but through a structured network, for Xers, more casual, direct and somewhat skeptical, and for Millennials, their style is casual, direct and eager to please
- Work and family are kept separate for Traditionalists, work comes first for Boomers, Xers value work/life balance while Millennials blend personal life into work
- Traditionalists believe loyalty to the organization comes first, for Boomers the importance and meaning of work is first, Xers value individual goals over all else, while Millennials give their loyalty to the people involved in their individual projects
- Traditionalists seldom question authority, Boomers respect power and accomplishments, Xers want rules that are flexible, while Millennials value autonomy and are less inclined to pursue formal leadership roles

- For Traditionalists, work is an obligation, for Boomers an exciting challenge, for Xers a contract and for Millennials a means to an end

The Solution:

- Provide on-going training in communication skills for management and employees that teaches how to communicate with different behavioral styles and values, using *Dynamic Communications* and *Your Attitude is Showing* seminars
- Recognize and appreciate the difference among generational workers
- Provide training in diversity issues, using the *Discovering Diversity Profile*
- Examine policies and practices to ensure they are appropriate for all employee age groups
- Provide an environment that allows for all employees to contribute
- Remember that generational workers share the need for dignity and respect, fair treatment and the belief they are making a significant contribution to the organization
- Create multifunctional teams pairing new hires with more experienced workers
- Do not stereotype employees and avoid derogatory labels

"...every generation brings its own set of rules and behaviors with them into the business world and nobody seems to know what's the standard anymore."
~Perrin Cunningham, *Business Etiquette for Dummies*

~ THE SKILLS GAP ~

Short on talent. Here's why:

~ The U.S. educational system lacks adequate student preparation especially in math, science and technological skills and has an overabundance of students who have an attitude of entitlement

~ Higher skills and huge labor market in competing countries

~ "The real problem is not one of finding bodies---it is a problem of finding the right skills set.
~Stacey Jarrett Wagner, NAM

~ "It comes down to the fact that companies aren't training their own people."
~Peter Cappelli, The Wharton School

~ "Ability will never catch up with the demand for it."
~Malcolm Forbes

"Companies must either invest in their human capital value chain and continuously build competency or lose their competitive advantage. Either drive the truck or serve as road kill."

~Vince Serritella, Grainer, Inc.

~ THE SKILLS GAP ~

Definition: When the number of workers who can perform at a certain level of competency cannot meet requirements of a position they have applied for or presently hold.

The Situation:

Based on input from 800 respondents to the Deloitte/ National Association of Manufacturers 2005 Skills Gap Report, we learn that:

- 81% said they are currently facing a moderate or severe skills gap
- 53% indicated at least 10% of their total positions currently remain unfilled due to a lack of qualified candidates
- 39% reported a shortage of unskilled production employees
- 90% indicated a moderate to severe shortage of qualified skilled production employees
- 65% of all respondents reported a moderate to severe shortage of scientists and engineers
- 60% of all new jobs in the 21st century will require skills that only 20% of the current workforce possesses

- Jobs previously categorized as unskilled labor jobs now require at least basic reading and some math ability
- One-third of U.S. companies will lose 11% or more of their workforce to retirements by 2008
- Incoming workers with inadequate skills are the greatest challenge to organizational performance
- The most crucial skills needed by employees over the next three years are strong basic employability skills, technical skills, reading, writing and communication skills, the ability to work as a team, strong computer skills, the ability to read and translate drawings/diagrams/flow charts, mathematical skills, strong supervisory skills, innovation and creativity skills and fluency in the English language
- When asked what percentage thinks that the following issues will be affected by an aging workforce, a Michigan Ross School of Business survey found that 43% of respondents believe corporate culture will be affected, 42% said quality of talent, 31% said the ability to compete, while 31% said the ability to recruit will be affected
- Employers who invested an average of $1,595 on training per person have a gross profit margin 24% higher that companies that spent just $128, according to an ASTD study

The Disconnect:

- U. S. education K-12/college student preparation is inadequate
- A mere 31% of college graduates can read a complex book and extrapolate from it

- The National Science Teachers Association reports that just 70,000 engineers graduated from U.S. schools of engineering in 2004 compared to India's 350,000 and China's 600,000 (Note: China and India may have less stringent requirements than the U.S.)
- An exodus of baby boomers with years of accumulated experience leaving the workforce. Most damaging loss is with the exit of "critical talent" which is defined as individuals and groups who possess highly developed skills, have an in-depth knowledge of work and know how to make things happen within an organization. They drive a disproportionate share of company's performance and have a higher effect on company's bottom line. These are known as our "A" performers
- Ineffective approaches to talent management
- Types of skills gaps presently in organizations of the 200 ASTD members who responded to their 2005/2006 study:
  - Leadership/executive-level skills
  - Managerial/supervisory skills
  - Communication/interpersonal skills
  - Basic skills
  - Technical/It/system skills
  - Sales Skills
  - Customer service skills
  - Process and project management skills

The Solution:

- Develop and practice talent management initiative
- Benchmark skill competencies required for each position

- Use skills/competency assessments such as *Prevue* (as part of the hiring process), which measures how fast a person can react to new challenges correctly
- Identify the key performance factors necessary for optimum performance for each job role and communicate these expectations to each employee
- Increase basic skills training among employees who have deficiencies
- Provide mentors for new employees
- Give incentives and adjust work schedules for employees who are furthering their skills/education
- Provide continual opportunities for additional training
- Develop strong intern programs to identify potential hires
- Provide tuition reimbursement for employees who return to school/college to complete or further their education
- Establish a skills-sharing culture so skills are not lost when an employee leaves

tion beyond the avera
: SKILLED b : befittin
some knowledge of fac
ed•u•ca•tion \ ,e-jə-'kā·
educating or of being
knowledge and develc
man of little ∿〉 **2 :**
of teaching and learn
n'l\ *adj* — ed•u•ca•ti

"The illiterate of the 21st century will not be those who cannot read and write, but those who cannot learn, unlearn, and relearn."

~ Alvin Toffler

"People who cannot invent and reinvent themselves must be content with borrowed postures, second hand ideas, fitting in instead of standing out."

~Warren Bennis

~ TRUST ~

WHAT'S TRUST GOT TO DO WITH IT???

"Trust is the social glue that holds things together. It allows us to engage in social and commercial ventures. You can't contract everything. We develop relationships that are based on trusting that things will work out."

~Maurice E. Schweitzer

"We firmly believe that the primary driver (to employee loyalty) is directly related to the degree of trust they have in the person who supervises them."

~Rob Ward, Synovus Financial Corp.

"The ability to establish, grow, extend and restore trust with all stakeholders---customers, suppliers, investors, and co-workers---is the critical leadership competency in the new global economy."

~Stephen M. R. Covey

"What is trust? I could give you a dictionary definition, but you know it when you feel it. Trust happens when leaders are transparent, candid, and keep their word. It's that simple."

~Jack Welch

~ TRUST ~

Definition: Trust is the reliance on the integrity, strength, and ability of a person or thing.

The Situation:

- Trust is the foundation for all we do no matter the time, place or situation
- Female executives rate the level of trust at their workplaces lower than do male executives
- Trust between management and workers has declined at three out of four workplaces over the past two years (a Manchester Consulting study)
- A Watson Wyatt 2002 study found that organizations that possess a high degree of trust outperform low trust organizations by nearly three times as much
- People and organizations are more inclined to do business with those they trust rather than those they like
- Organizations with a high degree of trust instill greater loyalty in their employees while maintaining or improving their employee retention rate

- The Canadian Institute for Advanced Research reports that trust toward management is valued at $500,000 when the most trustworthy and least trustworthy managements are compared
- Organizations with a low trust factor find it more difficult to attract top talent

The Disconnect:

- A study by Paul Bernthal for DDI found that almost 47% of the respondents agreed that lack of trust is a problem within their organizations
- A Harris/Franklin Covey Poll found that a mere 15% of 23,000 respondents felt they worked in a high-trust environment while just 20% fully trusted the organization they worked for; just 13% have high-trust, highly cooperative working relationships with other groups or departments
- Symptoms of a trust-deficient organization include low initiative, an active "rumor mill," a high fear factor, turf wars and defensive behaviors
- A recent Watson Wyatt Work USA study found that 72% of employees believe their immediate bosses act with integrity and honesty, but just 56% believe the same of top management
- A study by Walker Information found that just 55% of all respondents say they would recommend their organization to others as a good place to work
- 52% of respondents to the above study said they would be labeled "troublemakers" if they reported unethical behavior
- Employers lose trust by lying or telling half-truths; acting inconsistently in what they say or do; by withholding information; "passing the buck;"

sending mixed messages and making excuses or blaming others for mistakes

The Solution:

- Provide a 360-degree feedback instrument to assess the level of trust in organizational relationships
- Develop an action plan to practice trust building behaviors that include dependability/reliability/consistency/support/cooperation and open and honest communication techniques
- Be honest, maintain integrity at all times
- Do the right thing regardless of personal risk or loss
- Show respect for others
- Make communication a top priority by sharing goals, information, strategies and vision
- Provide surveys on a regular basis that allow employees to sound off about their needs and to determine whether or not the behaviors of the leaders support the company's values
- Offer training on earning endorsement with the use of the *Global Model* as described in *"The Ripple Effect"* book by Judy Suiter
- Provide training in diversity issues with the DVD, *"Meet on Common Ground"*

~ WORK/LIFE BALANCE ~

"In the seventies, we were told we could do it all. We can't do it all. To have a work-life balance...YOU have to make it happen."

~Kim Walton

WHAT THE GENERATIONS ARE SAYING ABOUT WORK-LIFE BALANCE:

Generation X: "Give me balance now, not when I'm sixty-five!"

The Millennials: "Work isn't everything; I need flexibility so I can balance all my activities."

Baby Boomers: "I need balance, I need more time. I need to find meaning for myself."

The Traditionalists: "I need to work less as I have other things I want to do."

"The challenge of work-life balance is without question one of the most significant struggles faced by modern man. I've surveyed thousands of audiences about their greatest personal and professional challenges. Life balance is always at or near the top."

~Stephen R. Covey

~ WORK/LIFE BALANCE ~

Definition: Work-life balance is the achievement an individual feels when multiple responsibilities such as work and family come together to allow one to successfully find an equilibrium that permits the sense of satisfaction, physical well-being, and also includes a sense of accomplishment by a job well-done.

The Situation:

- We are connected 24/7, sometimes 365/24/7 in which personal time is often sacrificed to the workplace and professional obligations
- 1.7 million Americans hold extreme jobs caused by globalization, BlackBerries, Type A personalities and 70-hour work weeks
- Workers in the United States spend 20% more time on the job now than in 1970
- With dual income households, women, more than men, report stress related to work-life balance issues (60% of all women now work outside the home)
- According to a Harvard/McGill University study workplace policies for families in the U.S. are weaker than those of all high-income countries and

many middle-and-low income countries
- Despite available technological advances, workers are frustrated with multi-tasking expectations, time constraints and unclear priorities

The Disconnect:

- A Family and Work Institute (FWI) study found 1 in 3 U.S. workers are chronically overworked, while 54% report feeling overwhelmed by their workload
- More than 1/3 of all workers were not planning to use their full vacation leave while 50% of executives in the FWI study did not plan on taking a vacation
- 50% of top talent is heading for the door and replacement costs can be in the six figures range
- American workers average approximately 10 paid holidays per year as opposed to 25 for British workers and 30 for German workers
- 20% of American workers stay in touch with the office when on vacation
- Americans work 12 weeks more a year in total hours than Europeans; in 2006, the U.S. employee averaged 1,804 hours of work
- A Center for Creative Leadership study found that 50% of respondents said they had too little time for personal interests or relationships
- The Bureau of Labor Statistics reports that in 1900, 80% of American children had a working father and a stay-at-home mother; by 1999, the figure had dropped to just 24%
- 86 million American workers do not get a single day off to care for a sick child while 77% of work-

ers in a recent study by ComPsych reported going to the office when they themselves are sick
- The number of children home alone after school is in the millions
- Nearly 25% of working dads feel work is negatively impacting their relationship with their children, 48% said they missed a significant family event at least once in the last year and nearly 20% have missed four or more

The Solution:

- Provide time management training and/or assessments such as the *Time Mastery Profile* or the *Coping with Stress and Conflict Profile*
- Establish strong, specific work-life balance policies that allow for reduced working time, flexible hours and work locations along with work schedules that are compatible with school calendars
- Consider offering term-time working so that one parent can be home when school is not in session
- Keep the lines of communication open between employees and their immediate supervisors
- As the leader or manager, lead by example with strong work-life balance practices

~ WORKPLACE READINESS ~

ARE THEY SMARTER THAN A FIFTH GRADER???

A recent study by The Conference Board finds that over 42.4% of employer respondents rate the overall preparation of high school students for the entry-level jobs they fill as "deficient."

"Before anything else, preparation is the key to success."

~Alexander Graham Bell

~ WORKPLACE READINESS ~

Definition: All employees have the necessary skills to execute basic job requirements.

Note: We have already addressed the crucial skills gap that represents one of the largest concerns for organizations today. However, I believe that the following information is so vital in understanding the urgency of what we all face: the dearth of employees who actually possess what we call basic and applied skills. Among these skills is the ability to communicate and work with others, to demonstrate problem-solving abilities, and to have a sense of self-direction along with a strong work ethic. Companies have been willing to pay for ongoing advanced training, but not for basic skills. Most employers tend to think when people are born with a mouth and two ears, communication skills are innate, but that's not been my experience at all.

The Situation:

The basic and applied skills needed by high school graduates for successful entry-level job performance in order of rank from The Conference Board's *"Are They Really Ready to Work?"* Study, 2006 are:

- Written Communications
- Professionalism/Work Ethic

- Critical Thinking/Problem Solving
- Oral Communication
- Ethics/Social Responsibility
- Reading Comprehension
- Teamwork
- Diversity
- Information Technology Application
- English Language

Note: The majority of employer respondents (55.2%) reported they do not test new hires in basic skills.

The Disconnect:

The following deficiencies of new hires were noted by the above study:

- Written Communications 80.9%
- Professionalism/Work Ethic 70.3%
- Critical Thinking/Problem Solving 69.6%
- Oral Communications 52.7%
- Ethics/Social Responsibility 44.1%
- Reading Comprehension 38.4%
- Teamwork/Collaboration 34.6%
- Diversity 27.9%
- Information Technology Application 21.5%
- English Language 21.0%
- Increased training costs to bring new hires to acceptable employee levels
- Costs of turnover to replace unprepared workers

The importance of Applied Skills over the next five years will increase by:

- Critical Thinking/Problem Solving 77.8%
- Information Technology 77.4%
- Teamwork 74.2%
- Creativity/Innovation 73.6%
- Oral Communications 65.9%
- Professionalism/Work Ethic 64.4%
- Written Communication 64.0%

The Solution:

- Employers may need to test for basic skills proficiencies such as reading, comprehension, analytical problem-solving skills
- Employers may want to investigate assessment tools available such as *SELECT* for use in pre-screening applicants

~ WORKPLACE STRESS ~

Overheard in the Break Room:

~ "Since the reorganization, nobody feels safe."

~ "Drop everything and get me some information on a major reorganization initiative."

~ "I get over 300 emails on a daily basis."

~ "We're so backed up, I'm working 24/7 to get things done."

~ "I was up all night with a sick child."

~ "My BlackBerry controls my life and the network is down again!"

~ "You want what, when?"

"Managers are the key holders of corporate culture. They perpetuate it. While stress management techniques like yoga are great, if your boss is draconian, exercise is not going to help."

~ Michael Peterson

~ WORKPLACE STRESS ~

Definition: Workplace stress is an excess of pressure when workers feel out of balance/control over time, work issues/ relationships and encroachment on their personal time. Stress undermines performance, is costly to employers and causes illness among employees.

(Job stress can also be defined as the harmful physical and emotional responses that occur when the requirements of the job do not match the capabilities, resources, or needs of the worker. Job stress can lead to poor health and even injury.)

The Situation:

- Three out of every four American workers say their work is stressful caused by various reasons such as the physical environment, organizational practices, specific work factors, workplace changes or interpersonal relationships
- Bureau of Labor statistics show that workers who take time off work because of stress will be absent for about 20 days, while a study from Health and Safety Executive reports that each case of stress-related ill health leads to an average of 30.9 work-

ing days lost
- In the United States, over half of the 550 million working days lost each year because of absenteeism are stress-related with the costs to organizations estimated at $200 billion per year
- Employees who are fairly treated at work were nearly one-third less likely to be stressed (See Finland 19 yr. study of 6400 government workers.)
- Nearly half of large American organizations offer employees stress management training along with Employee Assistance Programs
- Less stress occurs when employees are involved and empowered in organizational functions
- Stress is not all bad; a certain amount contributes to higher creativity and productivity
- Job stress can be traced to specific work factors such as excessive workloads, tedious tasks, unreasonable performance demands with long hours and low pay
- Additional causes of job stress can be the physical environment, organizational practices such as conflicting job demands, workplace changes with frequent turnover or fear of layoffs, and interpersonal relationships harmed by bullying, or subordinates or supervisors who are distant and uncommunicative
- The United Nations' International Labor Organizations has identified occupational stress as a "global epidemic"

The Disconnect:

- A Northwestern National Life survey reports that 40% of all workers surveyed believe their job is very or extremely stressful, while 25% view their jobs as the number one stressor in their lives

- Inscape Publishing, Inc. reports as many as 25% of all workers suffer from some stress-related, on the job problem
- 60% of lost workdays can be attributed to stress with over one million American workers calling in sick per day because of stress-related causes
- Work related stress costs the American economy more than $300B per year in terms of absenteeism, productivity, employee turnover and related expenses
- The British Medical Journal reports that chronic job stress is a risk factor for heart and vascular diseases
- Pressures surpass employees' ability to handle them
- Research shows that stress affects women more than men, and that they are more likely to report burnout, experience stress-related illnesses, and have a desire to resign from the workplace

The Solution:

- Identify and eliminate the stressor through discussions, surveys and employee perceptions of job conditions
- Clearly define employee's roles and responsibilities
- Provide coping and stress management training programs such as the *Coping and Stress Profile®,* a self-directed learning tool, that gives valuable feedback by focusing on the relationship among the four key life areas: Personal, Couples, Family

and Work
- Provide *Success Insights Management-Staff Reports* that identify employee behavior styles and that suggest techniques to better communicate with others' behavior styles and *Success Insights Personal Interests, Attitudes & Values Reports* to better understand different values perspectives
- Organizational change is necessary for the reduction of workplace stress by improving communication, consulting your employees on decisions that affect their jobs, providing rewards and incentives for work performance, and fostering a work environment that is non-threatening
- Provide opportunities for social interaction among employees

"The greatest weapon against stress is our ability to choose one thought over another."

~William James

~ CHANGE AGENTS ~

'In a time of drastic change it is the learners who inherit the future. The learned usually find themselves equipped to live in a world that no longer exists."

~Eric Hoffer

"Life is like riding a bicycle. To keep your balance you must keep moving."

~Albert Einstein

"Life is like an ever-shifting kaleidoscope---a slight change, and all patterns alter.

~Sharon Salzberg
Cofounder, Insight Meditation Society

"We now accept the fact that learning is a lifelong process of keeping abreast of change."

~Peter Drucker

~ CHANGE AGENTS ~

Definition: A person, an event, a condition or mechanism that causes major social, cultural or behavioral changes.

The Disconnect: Time and money often preclude the necessity for keeping abreast of new and innovative technological changes that are available, usually just a click away on your computer or other communication devices.

- Huge costs to businesses and organizations as a recent survey found that 87% of 800 employees in diverse organizations accessed various websites at least once a day, with over 43% reporting access for personal interests
- Defamation and distortion of correct information concerning companies and/or employees
- Work-related issues are openly discussed, issues that should be discussed or handled in-house
- Online bullying
- Copyright and trademark infringement

Listed below are just a few of what we, here at CEI, call Change Agents which have evolved from the expansion of the Internet and technological changes. (It is difficult to get a true number on the amount of users on various sites as this tends to change minute by minute.)

GOOGLE

Google actually began as a research project in 1996 by Larry Page and Sergey Brin, both of whom were students at the time at Stanford University in California. It was incorporated in 1998 and is the most popular search engine on the web. They acquired YouTube in 2006. Google offers online Images, Videos, GMail (free email service with mobile access), Maps, Patent Search, Google News, Google Book Search, Google Earth and as Google reports, they go "on and on."

Google (In Just 10 Short Years!)

<u>Number of searches per day:</u>
1998	10,000
1999	500,000
2008	235 Million

<u>Number of web pages in Google Index:</u>
1998	26 Million
2004	4.3 billion
2008	1 Trillion

<u>Number of Employees:</u>
1998	8
1999	41
2008	19,604

- **By May 2000, language versions were made available in the following translations: French, German, Italian, Swedish, Finnish, Spanish, Portuguese, Dutch, Norwegian and Danish**

- In September 2000, Chinese, Japanese and Korean languages added

- May 2008, Bulgarian, Croatian, Czech, Danish, Finnish, Hindi, Norwegian, Polish, Romanian added to language versions which now totals 23 including original Google language of English

---

MYSPACE: www.myspace.com

This is a popular social networking website that offers teenagers and adults a network for connecting with friends, sharing personal profiles, blogs, photos, music and videos.

- Founded in 2003, MySpace has 300 employees
- Ranked as the 3rd top site in the U.S. and the 6th worldwide.
- MySpace is presently available in 15 languages
- By June 2008, the number of visits to their site was estimated at 117.6M

FACEBOOK: www.facebook.com

This social network is a rival of MySpace. It is a free-access website, privately owned and operated by Facebook, Inc.

- Launched in 2004, by Mark Zuckerberg, a student at Harvard University at the time
- By June, 2008, Facebook had an estimated 132.1M visitors with the user age between 25 and older
- Currently, there are more than 100M active users worldwide
- Facebook offers more than 55,000 regional, professional, collegiate and high school networks
- It is ranked 5th on the list of top U.S. websites and 8th globally

More and more companies are turning to social networks such as Facebook to find candidates and more importantly, to vet candidates.

SECOND LIFE: www.secondlife.com

Second Life is a tremendously popular multiplayer online role-playing game in which an increasingly number of people interact in a virtual world. One can adopt an avatar and develop a whole new persona outside the real world.

- Founded in 2003 by Linden Labs, a software company
- By 2007, Second Life had about 9.6 million users called "residents"
- Approximately 45,000 residents are logged on at any given time
- Residents use Linden Dollars to purchase avatars
- Linden Dollars are purchased with the user's actual

currency or the exchange of services
- Avatars allow residents to create an alter ego which can be altered according to one's wishes with, of course, the use of more Linden Dollars

A plethora of companies have been attracted to this site and have set up businesses by buying islands from which to market their products. My caveat on this site: it all comes with a price and will cause one to escape the real world while losing much of life's experiences in the real world. And isn't this what really matters?

CRAIGSLIST: www.craigslist.org

Craigslist is a forum for jobs, housing, consumer goods and many social activities.

- Incorporated as a non-profit in 1999
- As of 2007, there were more than 40 million users each month
- Craigslist has expanded into approximately 500 cities in 50 countries
- They operate with just 25 employees, headquartered in a Victorian style house in the San Francisco Bay area.
- Craigslist receives more than 2 million job listings each month

---

YOUTUBE: www.youtube.com

Describing itself as "the world's most popular online community, YouTube allows users to upload, view and share video clips across the Internet through websites, mobile devices, blogs and emails

- This site was founded in 2005
- Acquired by Google in 2006
- As of January 2008, there were approximately 79 million users viewing 100M videos.
- It has become a huge marketing tool for companies, entertainment organizations and even political candidates.

WIKIPEDIA: www.wikipedia.com

Looking for quick information? Check out Wikipedia, a web-based, free content encyclopedia launched by Jimmy Wales and Larry Sanger in 2001, which has become one of the largest reference sites on the internet. There is a caveat: Wikipedia is written collaboratively by volunteers from all around the world; therefore, it would be best to verify any information collected from this site with additional support data. Also, Wikipedia articles are never complete as they are constantly edited and improved overtime.

- Created in 2001
- As of 2008, Wikipedia had approximately 684M visitors to its site.

- Wikipedia also provides links to guide users to related pages with additional information

---

iPODs

This portable media player needs little introduction to most people today. As a recent ad claimed, one can access millions of songs, thousands of movies and hundreds of games

- The first generation iPod was introduced in 2001
- The sixth generation introduced in 2007 with an update in 2008
- Three years ago, 304,000 iPods were sold
- By the second quarter of 2007, 8,100,000 were in the hands of consumers.
- According to Wikipedia, iPods have become acceptable as business devices such as delivering business communications and staff training.
- iPods are also gaining popularity in educational uses.

ARE YOU LINKEDIN FOR CHANGE???

LinkedIn: www.LinkedIn.com

LinkedIn is a hugely popular business-oriented social network that was launched in 2003. Its purpose is to allow for registered users to list and maintain contact detail of people they know and trust in business. In turn, they build connections to other registered users' contacts. This "gated-access approach" leads to a contact network where introductions may lead to increased business opportunities, career development, advice from experts in many areas, and job opportunities. Think of this site as your "Rolodex'" online.

Here are some data on LinkedIn:

- Has grown to 26M members in 5 years
- Approximately 150 industries are represented by its membership
- Increased its membership by 100% in the last year
- Experienced 361% growth in the number of page views between April 2007 and April 2008
- Signs up one new member every two seconds
- Half of its membership is outside the United States
- The present focus is on developing the market in the UK
- Is looking at other European markets and recently launched a site in Spain with additional growth in Latin America
- The largest growth area is in financial services as members are using LinkedIn to find experts (they can trust) for investment opportunities
- Membership is free, although some members who are involved in business developing and recruiting purchase a Premium membership

---

AMAZON KINDLE

The Kindle, developed by Amazon.com, is an e-book reader, an embedded system for reading electronic books. Using an electronic paper display with a LCD side scroller, the Kindle can be used without a computer.

- Launched in November 2007
- Books are delivered to your reader in less than 1 minute after purchase
- More than 170,000 books are available for this wireless reading device
- Top U.S. and many international newspapers can be delivered through this syste
- Holds over 200 titles
- Wikipedia and the ability to email Word docs and pictures are added features

This device is said by some people to be "the future of book reading." Some bibliophiles will have a hard time agreeing with that statement. Can an electronic device really replace the actual page turning with a hardback or paperback book?

~ SOMETHING EXTRA... ~

On the following page, use the designations below to test your generational knowledge:

     a. Millennials   c. Traditionalists

     b. Boomers   d. Generation Xers

~ GENERATIONAL QUIZ ~

_____ 1. The satisfaction of a job well done.

_____ 2. "Give me balance now, not when I'm 65!"

_____ 3. "Whatever it takes; let's get it done!"

_____ 4. They have been labeled the "Me Generation."

_____ 5. "Work isn't everything; I need balance in my life.

_____ 6. "I can have it all."

_____ 7. "I know I wasn't here at 8:00, but I got the workdone."

_____ 8. Freedom is the ultimate reward.

_____ 9. They abhor the concept of dues paying.

_____ 10. Their career goals included building a legacy.

_____ 11. Demand personal attention, efficiency and quick feedback.

_____ 12. Money, title, recognition, the corner office.

Answers: 1. c, 2. d, 3. c, 4. b, 5. a, 6. b, 7. a, 8. d, 9. d, 10. c, 11. a, 12. b

~ ADDITIONAL RESOURCES TO HELP WITH THE DISCONNECTS IN THE WORKPLACE ~

Communication:
Alessandra, Ph.D., Tony and Michael J. O'Connor, Ph.D., with Janice VanDyke. *People Smart*

Ernst, Ron. *Real Time Coaching*

Patterson, Kerry, Joseph Grenny, Ron McMillan, and Al Switzler. *Crucial Conversations, Tools for Talking When Stakes Are High*

Suiter, Judy. *Energizing People, Unleashing the Power of DISC and Exploring Values, Releasing the Power of Attitudes*

Connectivity:
Rath, Tom. *Vital Friends*

Employee Retention/Turnover:
Reichheld, Frederick F. *The Loyalty Effect, the Hidden Force Behind Growth, Profits, and Lasting Value*

Ethics:
www.globalethics.org The Institute for Global Ethics is an online source for news and information on ethics and current events.

www.businessethics.com The magazine of corporate responsibility.

Generational Differences:
Izzo, Ph.D., John and Pam Withers. *Values Shift, the New Work Ethic and What It Means for Business*

Lancaster, Lynne C. and David Stillman. *When Generations Collide*

Trust:
Suiter, Judy. *The Ripple Effect, How the Global Model of Endorsement Opens Doors to Success*

Work/Life Balance:
Seligman, Ph.D., Martin E.P. *Learned Optimism, How to Change Your Mind and Your Life*

Workplace Stress:
Dreher, Henry. *The Immune Power Personality, 7 Traits You Can Develop to Stay Healthy*

General Use:
www.audiotech.com Provides summaries of the most important and timely business books.

www.fastcompany.com A monthly publication that contains best practices, lessons learned and cases from cutting edge companies and entrepreneurs.

www.workforce.com Discussion, forums, solutions for many of your workforce problems.

(All books referenced above can be found on www. amazon.com.)

~ ABOUT THE AUTHOR... ~

Judy Suiter is founder and CEO of Competitive Edge, Inc., located in Peachtree City, Georgia, since its inception in 1981. Competitive Edge, Inc., is recognized internationally as a top human resource and training company specializing in candidate selection, executive development, team building, coaching and sales training. Judy has designed and conducted training programs for over 60,000 people in numerous organizations in both the US and in Europe. Her firm's motto is, "Be Daring, Be First, Be Different!"

A graduate of Middle Tennessee State University with a degree in Industrial and Personnel Psychology, she has over 640 hours of advanced behavioral and organizational training. Judy's belief that "learning is directly proportional to the amount of fun that people have" keeps her in constant demand as a trainer and speaker for national and international conferences and seminars.

Judy is the author if *Energizing People: the Power of DISC*, based on the behavioral theories of Dr. William Moulton Marston; *Exploring Values: Releasing the Power of Attitudes* based on Eduard Spranger's research on the six motivating values; *The Ripple Effect, How the Global Model of Endorsement Opens Doors to Success*, and *The Journey, Quotes to Keep Your Boat Afloat! Energizing People, Exploring Values*, and *The Ripple Effect* are available in German versions, while *Energizing People* and *Exploring Values* are currently published in a Swedish version. Ms. Suiter is the co-author of *The Universal Language DISC, A Reference*

Manual, currently in its tenth printing; Judy also contributed two chapters to the book, *The Pleasure and Quality of Life* published by John Wiley & Sons.

To purchase any of Ms. Suiter's books or to learn more about her organization, please access her website at www.competitiveedgeinc.com.

Judy Suiter, President
COMPETITIVE EDGE, INC.
PO Box 2418
Peachtree City, GA 30269

770.487.6460 phone
770.487.2919 fax
judy@competitiveedgeinc.com
www.competitiveedgeinc.com

Additional Information about Competitive Edge, Inc.

As a certified distributor of:

- TTI Performance Systems, Ltd.
- Inscape Publishing
- Brain Technologies Corporation
- Maximum Potential, Inc.
- HRD Press

Competitive Edge, Inc., can offer a variety of assessments and training programs to meet the challenges of the changing talent management issues in today's workplace.

Many of our assessments are available in multiple languages to serve global organizations.